To

From

CHANUKAH
A JOYOUS CELEBRATION

By Rabbi Daniel S. Wolk

Illustrated by Jo Gershman

Book design by Lesley Ehlers

Accompanying CD recorded by
The Western Wind Vocal Ensemble

Peter Pauper Press, Inc.
White Plains, New York

Recipes, and introductions thereto, are adapted from THE JEWISH HOLIDAY KITCHEN, REVISED AND EXPANDED by Joan Nathan, Copyright © 1988 by Joan Nathan, Reprinted by permission of Schocken Books, distributed by Pantheon Books, a division of Random House, Inc.

Musical Selections from *The Chanukkah Story* © 1991, sung by The Western Wind
from
Western Wind Records' Judaica Series
The Passover Story (WW 1800)
The Chanukkah Story (WW 1818)
Taste of Eternity, A Musical Shabbat (WW 1890)
The Birthday of the World: Yom Kippur (WW 1872)
The Birthday of the World: Rosh Hashanah (WW 1854)
Mazal Bueno: A Portrait in Song of the Spanish Jews (WW 1836)

Western Wind Records are available by calling 1-800-788-2187;
E-mail: recordings@westernwind.org
Or Web: www.westernwind.org

The editors have elected to spell the English transliteration of the Jewish holiday as "Chanukah."

CHANUKAH
A JOYOUS CELEBRATION

The Story of Chanukah

The elderly priest Mattathias stood in the shade of an olive tree near the village square of Modin, seventeen miles from Jerusalem. On a normal day the dull sound of stones pressing olives would be heard in the countryside—but this was not a normal day. A frown highlighted the wrinkles in Mattathias' weathered face. Silently, the Jews of Modin filed into the square where a wooden altar had been erected.

Mattathias thought back on his life: on the constant struggle to protect his faith from the onslaught of the Hellenistic culture. This was the enemy without. But the enemy also lurked within. Many Jews had adopted Hellenism. For instance, Jews wrestled naked in the gymnasium and, to disguise their identity, some of these athletes agreed to a painful operation to reverse their circumcision. Others wore Greek

dress and adopted Greek customs. Jews had left their agrarian lifestyle to trade with Greeks, and took on Greek names. The society had become divided between Hellenists and Hasidim. Mattathias, well aware of this desire to assimilate, lamented the loss of the uniquely Jewish heritage. But on this day in the year 168 BCE his musings centered on the political events leading up to Modin.

The history of Judaism had been (and still is) molded by the environment within which Jews live. In one epoch Judaism flourished with an independence that permitted fulfillment; at other times external forces imposed their own will on Jews and other minorities. In 332 BCE, when Alexander conquered Persia, the Jews of Judaea were permitted self rule. Alexander died nine years later, and Judaea became a battleground between Egypt and Syria. The Ptolemies of Egypt ruled until 198 BCE but were overthrown by the Syrian Selucids. When Antiochus IV came to power in 175 BCE the situation changed. Antiochus stamped coins with his image on the face of the coin and called himself Epiphanes, "The Great One."

Antiochus entered into battle with Judaism, intending to eradicate the religion. Widespread decrees negated worship on the Sabbath

or festivals. Circumcision was outlawed as well as reading from the
Torah. These prohibitions touched at the very heart of the spiritual
life of Judaism and threatened the continuation of the faith. Antiochus also commanded his subjects to worship pagan gods, bow down
to idols, and eat pig. Those who refused were sentenced to death,
often brutal in its execution. The names of Hannah and her seven
sons and the sage Eleazar stand out in this period as individuals who
refused to follow the edict of Antiochus. They became martyrs to their
conviction, meeting death by savage dismemberment and burning at
the stake.

Mattathias knew all this history. The single event that inflamed
his spirit, however, as he watched events unfold in the village square in
Modin that day, had taken place in the Hebrew month of Kislev (cor-
responding to December) in 168 BCE and centered on the Temple in
Jerusalem. Of all sites holy to the Jews, none could compare to the
Temple. On the festivals of Passover, Sukkot, and Shavuot, Jews from
nearby Judaea and distant Babylonia or Antioch made a pilgrimage to
the Temple. Bringing sacrifices—a pigeon, a sheep, the finest fruits of
the field—the pilgrims would ascend the Temple Mount, enter the

outer courtyard, and offer their gifts to God. The Levitical priests would accept these offerings on God's behalf, and the weary journeyers would return home fulfilled in worship, received by God.

Antiochus knew that if the Temple were no longer accessible Judaism would be severed at its source. Therefore, Antiochus sent mercenaries to the Temple, destroyed the sacred vessels, and scattered pigs' blood on the Holy of Holies. Profaning the altar, Antiochus installed a statue of the Greek deity Zeus and dedicated the Temple to this pagan god. To celebrate, "The heathen filled the temple with riot and reveling. On the king's birthday every month the Jews were taken to share in the sacrifice, and when the festival of the Dionysia came round they were compelled to wear ivy wreaths for the procession in honour of Dionysus." *(1 Macc. 6:4, 7, 8)* (The historical account is found in the Apocrypha, the Books of Maccabees.)

The zealot Mattathias felt helpless in the wake of these atrocities but he was pulled into the fray on that day in Modin when his musings were interrupted by a garrison of Selucid troops commanded by Apelles. Apelles, his sword swinging in the folds of his tunic, entered the square, followed by his soldiers. A hush enveloped the people of

Modin as Apelles ascended a makeshift altar. Mattathias tensed, digging his sandals into the sand, as the Selucid commander swaggered to the highest point and fixed his eyes upon Mattathias and his sons: Judah, Johanan, Simon, Eleazar, and Jonathan. Mattathias' gaze never wavered as Apelles' voice boomed out toward the vineyard: "You are a ruler, great in this city, upheld by sons and brothers. I ask you, therefore, to be the first to carry out the King's command, as all the nations have done and all the people of Judah and those who remain in Jerusalem. Then you and your sons will be honored with silver, gold and many gifts." *(1 Macc. 2:17,18)*

"Carry out the king's command!" Mattathias knew the meaning of those words. He was being commanded to come forth and sacrifice a pig—to serve as a role model, and to enlist those who lived in the environs of Modin. Another victory for the God Zeus. If Mattathias stepped forth, all would follow. But, resolute, Mattathias held his place. Once more Apelles commanded: "Be the first to come forward." Syrian and Jew alike waited for a further response. Mattathias looked at his own people, cowed by the army of Apelles. Then he faced the Commander and the words that flowed from Mat-

tathias' mouth were destined to enter the annals of immortality.

"If all the nations that are within the king's dominions obey him by forsaking, every one of them, the worship of their fathers, and have chosen for themselves to follow his commands, yet will I and my sons and my brethren walk in the covenant of our fathers. Heaven forbid that we should forsake the Law and the ordinances; the law of the king we will not obey by departing from our worship either to the right hand or to the left." *(1 Macc. 2:19-22)* Mattathias' words cut through the heavy air in the Judaean Hills like a sword piercing his enemy. The villagers huddled together, aware that there was no turning back. Mattathias had taken on the empire.

No one expected the next move in the drama. A lone Jew came forward, approached the altar, and offered to sacrifice the pig. Before he could take the knife, Mattathias leaped onto the platform and slew the Jew. The rebellion was under way.

Over the next years, Mattathias and his sons waged war against the Selucids. How could a meager band of farmers battle with the might of an empire? The Selucids had a battle-hardened army with infantry, chariots, camel and elephant units, men capable of using

javelins, swords, a machine that hurled stones, battering rams, bows, spears. It was reminiscent of David and Goliath, with the Jews armed only with slings used in the fields to ward off stray animals, the mace (a primitive stone weapon mounted on a wooden handle), pitchforks, and scythes.

Judah and his men fought at night, employed strike-and-run techniques, relied on the element of surprise against a set army, gathered intelligence information from women living in the villages. Messages were passed from village to village by smoke signals, runners, children. Throughout history world powers have been brought down by guerilla tactics—especially when the local population is inspired by the conviction of their faith. And the faith of these zealots was unswerving; it was their most powerful weapon.

When Mattathias died, leadership shifted to Judah, who was known as The Maccabee. No one is certain of the derivation of the word Maccabee. Those with a flair for the dramatic picture Judah darting in and out of the Syrian camp waving a banner with the Biblical phrase *Mi Chamocha Ba Elim Adonai* (Maccabee), or "Who is like unto you, Oh Lord?" Or, perhaps the word reflects the similar

Hebrew word for hammer, describing the hammer-like blows Judah inflicted upon the Syrians. For those who prefer theories of physiognomy, Judah's head might have been shaped like a hammer.

Judah's band wrested many victories from the hands of the Selucids and slowly liberated Judaea. Finally, in 165 BCE, Judah's army arrived in Jerusalem and liberated the Temple, but a desolate wasteland greeted them. Animal residue soiled the altar and the courts were overgrown with weeds. Even the stones of the altar had been ruined. Slowly, the Temple was rebuilt and the moment of rededication arrived, on the 25th day of Kislev. "And they burned incense upon the altar, and they lighted the lamps that were upon the candlestick in order to give light in the temple. And they set loaves upon the table, and hung up the veils, and finished all the works which they had undertaken." *(1 Macc. 4:50-52)*

The final act of rededication involved lighting the Eternal Light, the symbol of Israel's everlasting faith. The light would be fueled with oil, but, according to legend, when the Maccabees searched in the storehouse they found only a single cruse of pure oil, sealed with the stamp of the High Priest, enough for one day. Miraculously the oil burned for eight days until a new supply could be located.

Although Judah's father, Mattathias, was not at the Temple in Jerusalem to rejoice with his sons, the Maccabees, the spark for that eternal light burning in the Temple had really been kindled in a village square years before—in a moment when one man spoke up for the right of his people to practice their religion. Mattathias' call to keep the faith still echoes from the village of Modin, resounding through centuries of Jewish history wherever the Jewish people have lived.

The Lights of Chanukah

When we think of Chanukah we immediately think of oil burning for eight days, but this may be only a legend. The story of the oil does not appear in the Books of Maccabees, although oil is mentioned in the Talmud several hundred years later. But even legends have an origin. Some say the eight lights were really Syrian spears that the Maccabees found on the ground when they came to rededicate the darkened Temple. Placing flax on top of each spear, Judah and his brothers lit the flax and, with the light of the eight spears, cleansed the Temple—thus the eight lights of Chanukah.

The eight days may also have been a delayed observance of the Autumn festival of Tabernacles (Sukkot). At Sukkot Jews would parade through the streets of Jerusalem carrying lights, and the festival had been postponed because of the war between the Maccabees and the Selucids.

A third theory traces the festival of light to a pagan custom when, at approximately the time of the winter solstice, lights were kindled to urge the return of sunlight. In the depth of winter, we have from ancient times encouraged the hope of light and of longer days.

A story: It was not easy to be the first man. Adam lacked predecessors who could instruct him in the ways of the world. A time arrived when Adam sensed the sun disappearing earlier and earlier. Some months before, Adam and his friend Eve had wandered in the Garden of Eden in early evening, becoming acquainted with the animals, sitting in the shade of the fig tree, swimming in the still waters of the River Pishon. Not any more. By five o'clock (although Adam did not own a watch!) the day grew dark and Adam feared the sun was vanishing. Soon Adam and Eve would dwell in darkness. Frightened, Adam fasted for eight days and waited. Waited. The days passed and then Adam sensed that the sun was slowly returning. The days were longer. To commemorate the return of the sun Adam designated an eight-day period in the winter as a festival of light. And from that time forth at the period when the days are drab, Chanukah is celebrated to remind us that, no matter how bleak life may appear, there

is always light if we have faith and confidence.

A legend? A delayed Sukkot? A celebration of the winter solstice? A passage from the Talmud? The sign of a faith that was kept burning? What are the origins of the lights of Chanukah? Do we know? And does it matter? At sunset, on the 25th of Kislev, usually falling in the month of December, the family gathers around the Chanukah menorah.

First, the oil or candles are placed in the menorah. Today we take for granted the process of kindling the lights, but what the actual order should be was a hotly debated topic in the first century of the common era. There were two Rabbis, Hillel and Shammai, who discussed this topic well into the night. You are cordially invited to visit a Rabbinic Academy and listen to the Chanukah discussion, and since you are seated on a hard wooden bench we will abbreviate the Rabbis' words.

A question was posed: "Should we light one light of Chanukah the first night and eight on the last night or reverse the order, lighting eight lights on the first night and descending to one on successive nights?"

Shammai replies, "My revered colleague, Rabbi Hillel, surely you would agree that we should proclaim the miracle in all its majesty. Light all eight oil wicks on the first night, that the people may know the scope of the triumph."

Hillel arranges the folds of his white robe and strokes his beard. "Rabbi Shammai, there is validity in what you say—but I disagree. The drama should build slowly, for the miracle did not occur in a single night. Let us begin with one light and build to eight."

The School of Hillel prevailed. One light was to be kindled on the first night—one light and the shamash which lights the other candles. Because of the shamash, every Chanukah menorah has nine lights. That ninth light, the shamash, travels along the row of oil wicks or candles, giving its light to the others.

The shamash occupies a regal position, slightly raised from the other lights, but the shamash also experiences a lonely life. It gives its light-until, one would think, the shamash would give away all of its light. What is left for the shamash? But the more the shamash gives, the brighter it burns and, by the eighth candle, the shamash bursts forth in all its brightness. What does this mean? Perhaps the more we

give to others, the greater we glow within ourselves. When we give we receive, and both the candle and the human spirit thrive by sharing with others, not by hoarding. That is the legacy of the shamash. That is one of the many wonders of Chanukah.

The oil wicks or candles are placed in the menorah from right to left as you face the candelabra. They are lit from left to right. In other words, the newest light is the first to be acknowledged. Today we light the menorah inside the home, but in ancient times it was the custom to light the menorah outside or, to protect it from the weather, hang the menorah on the doorpost opposite the mezuzah. This practice was a rejection of Antiochus' practice of forcing the Jews to build pagan altars in front of their homes. Placing the Chanukah lights outside the home was both poetic justice and the final blow to Antiochus' failed plan to subjugate the Jews.

When are the lights kindled? At sundown. If on the Sabbath, then before lighting the Sabbath candles. But Judaism remains a practical religion. What happens when an army is in the field at Chanukah and lights glowing in the darkness would reveal fortified positions? The Rabbis recently decreed that in such situations the

menorah might be lit in the morning to fulfill the commandment and
protect lives.

Today, many families have menorahs for each member of the
family. These may include a silver tree of life, brightly colored yellow,
red and blue train cars, or even a line of painted ceramic elephants
with Chanukah candles inserted into their backs.

Why the elephant, native to India, in a celebration set in Israel?
The answer lies in the ingenious way in which elephants were used by
the Selucid forces in their battle against the Maccabees. These lum-
bering beasts were the heavy armor of those days, the ancient forerun-
ners of the tank. Mounted on the backs of the elephants were warriors
ready to shower stones, spears, and javelins on Judah's helpless foot
soldiers.

In one famous battle the elephants descended on Judah's army,
and the Jews were paralyzed by fear. Suddenly Eleazar, Judah's
younger brother, summoned his courage, slipped under one of the
massive animals and shoved his sword into the unprotected underbelly.
The beast died, falling upon Eleazar, the first of Mattathias' sons to
be killed. But, inspired by the heroism of Eleazar, Judah's forces

returned to battle and claimed future victories.

Traditionally, Chanukah menorahs were made of clay: nine separate oil lamps (including the shamash) with wicks of flax, pine needles wrapped with absorbent cotton or, recently, pipe cleaners inserted into holes. Oil lamps certainly predate Chanukah, and can be traced back to 2,500 BCE. At first the oil lamps, crudely shaped by hand, resembled saucers. Gradually the lamps evolved from open bowls, (energy inefficient!) to pinched-in rims on which a single wick could rest. The primitive pottery oil lamp that gave light to the dark Israelite houses eventually became a work of art, molded into two parts and then joined together (energy efficient!) with only a small hole for the wick and a separate hole to pour in oil. In the early centuries of the Common Era oil lamps often included a menorah etched into the surface. The menorah could not have seven branches because that would represent the menorah in the Temple in Jerusalem. With flair, the artist designed many-branched menorahs, some flanked with incense shovel and shofar. Although these oil lamps now cost thousands of dollars in antiquity shops, and are valued collectors' items, anyone can purchase inexpensive replicas, place them in a line on the window sill, and

journey back into a distant time.

When oil is used in the menorah, olive oil remains the oil of choice. According to the Bible the olive tree was the finest of trees. Once upon a time the trees of the forest went to find a tree to be king of the trees. There was only one tree to ask: the olive tree. The tree refused but it still reigns among all the trees. Visit the Garden of Gethsemane on the Mount of Olives in Jerusalem and you will see the gnarled branches of a 20-foot wide tree 2,000 years old, still standing, still bearing fruit, covering the hillside with tranquil but elegant green and silver leaves.

Cut down, the olive tree puts out new shoots, symbolic of a people who constantly re-emerge from tragedy. The wood of the tree provides the finest timber for houses. The dried leaves are used for paper, the green leaves as fodder for livestock. When harvested, the olives are crushed by millstones eight tons in weight. The paste, spread on nylon mats threaded one on top of the other, is pressed. Nothing goes to waste. The remaining paste is used to make soap, or as a salve for ears. While the roasted kernels are rubbed on teeth as an antidote for toothaches, it is the oil that gives to the olive tree its greatest value.

The kings of Israel, Saul, David, and Solomon, were anointed with the finest oil, the first pressing or virgin oil. Honored guests were anointed with olive oil, and the lesser oil was rubbed on the body against chills, or swabbed on fruit trees to keep off pests. When the Romans and Crusaders marched on Jerusalem, the defenders of the city, stationed on the ramparts, dropped burning oil on the invaders. For those no longer fighting Crusaders, the most common use of olive oil is for light, and that relates to Chanukah.

So light up your eight oil lamps. Fill them with oil and watch the light flicker. Think of ancient times, for who can retell the things that befell us? Who? The answer dances in the light of the menorah.

With the menorah in place, and the wicks lit, the blessings are recited.

Baruch ata Adonai Eloheinu,
Melech haolam, asher kideshanu
Bemitsvotav, vetsivanu
Lehadlik neir shel Chanukah.

בָּרוּךְ אַתָּה, יְיָ אֱלֹהֵינוּ,
מֶלֶךְ הָעוֹלָם, אֲשֶׁר קִדְּשָׁנוּ
בְּמִצְוֹתָיו, וְצִוָּנוּ
לְהַדְלִיק נֵר שֶׁל חֲנֻכָּה.

Blessed is the Lord our God, Ruler of the universe, who hallows us
with His Mitzvot, and commands us to kindle the Chanukah lights.

Baruch ata Adonai Eloheinu,
Melech haolam, sheasa nisim
Laavoteinu bayamim hahaim
Bazeman hazeh.

בָּרוּךְ אַתָּה, יְיָ אֱלֹהֵינוּ,
מֶלֶךְ הָעוֹלָם, שֶׁעָשָׂה נִסִּים
לַאֲבוֹתֵינוּ בַּיָּמִים הָהֵם
בַּזְּמַן הַזֶּה.

Blessed is the Lord our God, Ruler of the universe, who performed
wondrous deeds for our ancestors in days of old, at this season.

On the first night only

Baruch ata Adonai Eloheinu,
Melech haolam, shehecheyanu
Vekiyemanu vehigianu
Lazeman hazeh.

בָּרוּךְ אַתָּה, יְיָ אֱלֹהֵינוּ,
מֶלֶךְ הָעוֹלָם, שֶׁהֶחֱיָנוּ
וְקִיְּמָנוּ וְהִגִּיעָנוּ
לַזְּמַן הַזֶּה.

Blessed is the Lord our God, Ruler of the universe, for giving us life, for sustaining us, and for enabling us to reach this season.

Families still light oil lamps but, as the centuries passed, the separate pottery lamps became less popular. In their place, a lamp called a bench type lamp emerged. This lamp, made of metal, consists of a flat bottom with wick holders and a back, often triangular in shape. In the seventeenth century, menorahs similar to the seven-branch menorah in the Temple became fashionable. The style, a single stem with branches emerging from the side, was crafted in bronze and silver and bore various motifs, from a coat of arms, to lions, to the branches of a meandering tree of life. These menorahs were also placed in

conspicuous places in the synagogue to enable passersby, away from home, to celebrate the festival.

The origins of the seven-branched menorah can be traced to Biblical times. About 3,200 years ago, Moses commissioned the first Hebrew artist, Bezalel, to design a menorah for the Tabernacle. Bezalel, searching his environment for inspiration, discovered the low-growing moriah plant, a form of sage. The moriah, with curled branches shooting off a single stem, formed a perfect model for the menorah. Carefully described in the Book of Exodus, the menorah is depicted in botanical terms with petals, cups, and branches similar to the moriah plant. Today the moriah grows wild in Israel and has been cultivated in Biblical Gardens. This is the menorah emblazoned on the shield of Israel. Because of its antiquity, the menorah is justifiably the most authentic symbol of the State of Israel, rather than the Star of David, which became popular only a century ago.

Titus carried the original menorah (made of pure gold) to Rome when his army conquered Judaea, but the symbol has continued, in the Sinai, in the heart, and in the observance of Chanukah.

Foods of Chanukah

*O*il may not burn in your Menorah, but the holiday meal should include some item baked in oil. For instance, Israelis celebrate the festival with doughnuts (sufganiyot); a recent doughnut zealot constructed a pyramid of thousands of sufganiyot. Some cultures fry fruit fritters, and in the United States the overpowering smell of potato pancakes (latkes) penetrates kitchen, dining room, and even closets.

A question: What is the origin of the potato pancake? The initial response is: "Potato pancakes came from my grandmother. She had this incredible recipe, and whenever I smell that delicious, greasy pancake frying I think of her!" Well, in Judaism many of our finest memories are linked to a Jewish grandmother—everything from potato pancakes to wisdom—but potato pancakes predate even Jewish grandmothers!

Potato pancakes began with Judith. Not any Judith. This particular woman lived around the time of the Maccabees, and her town was besieged by a Syrian army led by Holofernes. Normally a modest and shy widow, Judith offered to seek out Holofernes and save her people. With female guile she ventured to the Syrian's tent and, enamored with Judith, Holofernes invited her to enter. Our heroine prepared a dairy feast for Holofernes, featuring cheese pancakes. Thirsty from the cheese, Holofernes drank wine in excess and fell into a deep sleep. Judith cut off his head and paraded through the streets to the enthusiastic shouts of her people.

Over the years the cheese pancake became a potato pancake, although no one is certain why. Perhaps the cheese contained too high a cholesterol count! But from this story arises the tradition of eating potato pancakes. Judith's act also testified to the strength and courage of Jewish women, and it is for this reason that women are obligated to light Chanukah candles, an integral part of the Chanukah observance.

Joan Nathan's Potato Latkes

Joan Nathan, in *The Jewish Holiday Kitchen*, explains: *For American Jews intrigued with the gastronomic side of Judaism, Chanukah appears to be the preferred holiday. It is difficult to equal the taste of brown, crisp potato latkes. Can gefilte fish, matzah balls, haroset, or even hamantashen compare with them? Certainly not. Moreover, every latke lover seems to know how to make these potato pancakes—admirers of, say, gefilte fish may be forced to an outside source—and has strong opinions about them. One will swear by a medium grater, another by the larger variety, and modernists by the grater on the food processor. Some prefer pepper; others, salt. Some add apples; others, grated zucchini, carrots, or parsley. Some insist on grated and others on sautéed onions. And then, of course, there are the purists who contend that only old potatoes and bruised knuckles will do.*

Latkes have become a versatile delicacy. They can be made from buckwheat or potatoes with a touch of flour. They can be served for

breakfast, brunch, lunch, dinner, or as cocktail-party fare. They can be eaten plain or fancy, with sugar, applesauce, sour cream, or even chicken soup.

10 medium potatoes
2 medium onions
2 large or 3 medium eggs
1/4 cup unbleached all-purpose flour,
   breadcrumbs, or matzah meal
Salt and white pepper to taste
Vegetable oil

1. Peel the potatoes if the skin is coarse; otherwise, just clean them well. Keep them in cold water until ready to prepare the latkes.
2. Starting with the onions, alternately grate some of the onions on the large holes of the grater and some of the potatoes on the smallest holes. This will keep the potato mixture from blackening. Press out as much liquid as possible and reserve the starchy sediment at the bottom of the bowl. Return the sediment to the mixture. (The steel blade

of a food processor or the grating blade are less painful ways of grating the potatoes and the onions. The blade makes a smooth consistency and the grater a crunchy one.)

3. Blend the potato mixture with the eggs, flour, salt, and white pepper.

4. Heat 1 inch of oil in a frying pan. Drop about 1 tablespoon of mixture for each latke into the skillet and fry, turning once. When golden and crisp on each side, drain on paper towels. Serve with yogurt, sour cream, sugar, or applesauce.

8-10 servings

Joan Nathan's Sufganiyot (Jelly Doughnuts)

Joan Nathan explains: *Sufganiyot are descended from one of the oldest sweets known to mankind—Greek loukomades, a sweet fritter dipped in honey-and-sugar syrup. Loukomades were originally wheatcakes fried on an iron grill, then covered with grape-derived molasses. . . . The honey syrup used today as a coating was borrowed from the Turks; the cooking method has changed to deep-frying.*

2 tablespoons or packages dry yeast
4 tablespoons sugar
3/4 cup lukewarm milk
2-1/2 cups all-purpose flour
2 egg yolks
Pinch of salt
1 teaspoon cinnamon
1-1/2 tablespoons softened butter, at room temperature

Vegetable oil for deep frying
Plum, strawberry, or apricot preserves
Sugar for rolling

1. Dissolve the yeast and 2 tablespoons sugar in the milk. Let sit 10 minutes.
2. Sift the flour. Place it on a board and make a well in the center. Add the yeast mixture, the egg yolks, salt, cinnamon, and the remaining sugar. Knead well. Work the butter and knead until the dough is elastic.
3. Cover and let rise overnight in the refrigerator.
4. Sprinkle flour on the board. Roll the dough out to 1/8 inch. Cut out with a glass into rounds about 2 inches in diameter. Cover and let rise 15 minutes more.
5. With your hand form into a ball. Insert a teaspoon of jam; enclose completely.
6. Pour 2 inches of oil into a heavy pot and heat to 375°.
7. Drop the doughnuts in the oil, 4-5 at a time, turning when brown. Drain on paper towels.

8. Roll in granulated sugar and serve. You can make larger sufganiyot if you like. Whatever you decide, eat them immediately!

Makes 24

Jews from different lands enjoy a wide variety of meals at Chanukah in addition to potato latkes, favored by Ashkenazy Jews, and sufganiyot (doughnuts), a delicacy of Sephardic Jews. For instance, Yemenite Jews returned from a journey on the hot desert sands and made a carrot stew. The meal was financed by Yemenite children who sold a drink made from peach juice and hot potatoes. In Hungary the main course would be a fat goose and a garlic soup—rich and heavy!

Although Jews enjoyed the Chanukah feast, they gave special consideration to those who were poor and to the scholars in the community. In Turkey, affluent Jews baked pancakes and brought them to their neighbors in return for coins for the impoverished. In Bukhara, grateful parents placed coins inside cakes and distributed them to teachers, satisfying the needs of both the stomach and the mind.

The liturgy following the Chanukah meal includes this prayer of thanksgiving:

Oh God we offer thanks for the miracles, for the redemption, for the deeds of valor, for the deliverance and for the battles that You

performed for our fathers in those days at this time.

In the days of Mattathias the son of Yochanan, the High Priest, the Hasmonaean and his sons, there arose the wicked Greek kingdom against Your people Israel, with the hope of causing them to forget Your Torah and to turn them away from the laws that You ordain. You, in Your great mercy, stood by them in their difficult time. You defended their needs and judged them in their lawsuits. You avenged them and You turned over the mighty into the hand of the weak and the many into the hand of the few, people who were defiled into the hands of those who were pure and the wicked into the hand of those who are righteous and those who are insolent into the hand of those who busy themselves and study Your Torah. And You made for Yourself a great and sanctified name in Your world and for Your people Israel. You performed great salvation and redemption that is remembered even unto this day. Afterwards Your sons entered the Holy of Holies where You dwell and cleansed Your Temple, purified Your sanctuary, and lit lights in the courtyards of Your holy place. There they designated these eight days of Chanukah to give thanks and to praise Your great name.

The Dreidel

What is Chanukah without a dreidel? Made of hand-carved wood, glass, or ceramic, this spinning top delights young and old. The four-sided dreidel contains a Hebrew letter on each side: N (nun), G (gimmel), H (heh), SH (shin). The letters stand for "A great miracle happened there." In Israel the fourth letter is a P (peh) meaning "here." The dreidel game is a form of gambling. Each participant places a raisin, a walnut, a piece of chocolate, or a coin in a pot, and the dreidel spins. If the dreidel falls on the nun, the spinner loses; on the gimmel, he or she takes the entire pot; on the heh, half the pot; and on the shin, the spinner places a coin in the pot. There are many variations to this game, and participants are free to make their own rules.

The dreidel appears to be a frivolous game of chance, but there is a more somber backdrop. When Antiochus forbade Jews to study the

Torah or gather in synagogues in the second century BCE, the Jews continued to meet secretly in homes. A lookout would be stationed near the door and give warning when the Syrians were near. At the first alarm, the students, taking a dreidel which they kept close to them when they studied, would spin the top and pretend they were only playing a harmless game.

We cannot be certain that the dreidel dates to Antiochus; we do know the game was played in Germany in the Middle Ages. German children would spin a three-winged top called a trendel or werfel. Each wing had a German letter that signified a certain number in this European version.

Spinning the dreidel also has a religious component based in the mystical concept of *gematria* which reads hidden meaning in numbers. Each letter of the Hebrew alphabet has a numerical value. Aleph = 1, Bet = 2, Gimmel = 3, and so forth. The letters on the dreidel add up to 358. (Nun = 50, gimmel = 3, hey = 5, shin = 300). 358 is the numerical equivalent to the Hebrew word for Messiah, Moshiah. (Mem = 40, shin = 300, yud = 10, chet = 8). Children can enjoy the challenge of watching whose dreidel spins longest, or on what

letter the dreidel lands, and adults can believe that they are focusing on the Messiah and hastening his arrival. In this way the dreidel represents the universality of Chanukah.

Chanukah Gelt

*I*n the good old days gift-giving at Chanukah was easy. That was in the age before video games, New York Giants sweatshirts, and Barbie dolls. Instead, coins were given—Chanukah gelt. In its simplest form the child received a penny the first night, two cents on the second night, four cents on the third night, and so on. The doubling effect resulted in a grand total of $1.28 on the eighth night. As the child progressed in age and higher math he or she might hold out for a quarter the first night and receive $32.00 on the last night. When the child bargained for a beginning ante of $1.00, astute parents who wished to avoid the eventual $128.00 declared a moratorium! Today Chanukah gelt is limited to chocolate coins.

However, since the Middle Ages, the concept of giving coins at Chanukah has been part of the celebrations. At first, coins were given to scholars as a bonus to honor Judaism's love of learning. The

scholar existed on the bonus (similar to Wall Street bonuses—except in magnitude). Eventually, coins were also given to children as a reward for studying Torah.

The coins represented more than a financial gift. Throughout history the privilege of minting coins was extended only to independent nations. Following the rededication of the Temple, Mattathias' descendants, the Hasmonaeans, minted coins with symbols of the Temple emblazoned on one side. These coins continued through the time of Antigonus (First Century BCE) when Judah was once again subjugated.

The next period of coinage in Israel occurred in 132 CE when Bar Kochba led a revolt against the Romans. To stress Israel's dominance, the images on Bar Kochba's coins were stamped directly over the head of Caesar on old Roman coins. A palm tree, lulav, or the facade of the Temple replaced the head of the monarch. In 135 CE, when the revolt was suppressed, coinage ceased, until Ben Gurion proclaimed the State of Israel in 1948. Remembering past freedoms, Israel strikes a special coin every year at Chanukah. The motif of these coins ranges from the menorah (also found on the last of the Maccabaean coins) to

a coin celebrating the 200th anniversary of the U.S. Declaration of Independence.

In today's world we tend to forget the significance of Chanukah gelt, but throughout history the coins played an important role in reaffirming liberty.

Footloose in Jerusalem

Since the earliest of times pilgrims have journeyed to Jerusalem. In 1898, when the German Emperor, Kaiser Wilhelm II, entered the Holy City, he insisted on entering on horseback. Unfortunately, the entranceway, the Jaffa Gate, lacked both the width and height for mounted visitors. The Kaiser, befitting his position as Emperor, tore down a section of the wall and with full pomp rode into Jerusalem. Today, Mercedes and BMWs drive through the route fashioned by Wilhelm II.

In contrast, observe General Allenby on December 11, 1917, the second day of Chanukah. Allenby, poised at the city gates, brought a second Chanukah miracle— not another cruse of oil but Turkish surrender. England would rule Palestine and, in time, there would follow the Balfour Declaration and eventually the State of Israel.

The Jewish residents of Jerusalem lined the streets and clustered

on rooftops to witness General Allenby, this Christian descendant of the Maccabee spirit. The British General, unlike his German predecessor, dismounted and walked into the Old City, an act of respect admired by the Jerusalemites. Only the muffled footsteps of the General echoed through the dusty streets on that second day of Chanukah. Ascending the steps of the Citadel, he read a proclamation (which began: "To the inhabitants of Jerusalem the Blessed and the people dwelling in the vicinity . . . ") assuring that all faiths would be able to adhere to their sacred beliefs—setting the stage for the drama of a reborn Israel.

An editorial in *The Maccabean* exulted:

Faithful Jews were celebrating the Festival of Lights, the Maccabean victories of centuries long past, while in Palestine the British army took the citadel for which the Maccabees fought and in defense of which thousands of Jews in different periods of history gave up their lives. Jerusalem has fallen many times, but only of this time in the modern period may it be said that it has been delivered. . . .

In modern times, at Chanukah, Jews visit Modin, the humble village home of the Maccabees, at present a large and expanding settlement area. On the first day of Chanukah, before sunset, a bonfire is lit on the hillside and the Israeli flag flies above the land where the Hasmonaean revolution began. Young and old of the Maccabee sport associations, which hold a worldwide Olympic competition every four years, would often light torches in a bonfire. A torch passed from runner to runner in a relay race that began at Modin and concluded in Jerusalem. The light flashed along the route the Maccabees followed on their way to Jerusalem until the last runner entered Jerusalem on foot. The torch would pass on to Mt. Zion, the Western Wall, and would then be on an El Al flight to the United States, binding the two major Jewish communities in an unbroken bond.

Whether by a Maccabee, an Allenby, or a modern relay runner, the footsteps of history have always resounded on the stone pavements of Jerusalem.

Maoz Tsur

Of all the Chanukah songs, some lighthearted ("I Have A Little Dreidel") and others celebrating events in Judaea ("Who Can Retell"), the signature song for the holiday is Maoz Tsur, Rock of Ages. The words, by an Italian lyric writer named Mordecai (an acrostic of the first letter of each verse), were written in the thirteenth century. The melody, an amalgam of many cultures, approximates German folk music, probably from the Protestant Church but familiar to German synagogues in the eighteenth century. There may also be a connection to the music of Benedetto Marcello, the Venetian composer. In any event, it is often difficult to delineate the influences in much Jewish music, since the Jewish people have been exposed through history to many lands and cultures. The theme of Maoz Tsur, however, is clear: It emphatically relates how God has redeemed the Jews throughout history, whether in Egypt, Babylonia, Persia, or in Hellenist times.

Rock of Ages let our song
Praise Your saving power;
You, amid the raging foes,
Were our sheltering tower.
Furious they assailed us,
But Your arm availed us.
   And Your word
    Broke their sword
When our own strength failed us.
(Repeat last three lines.)

Kindling new the holy lamps,
Priests approved in suffering,
Purified the nation's shrine,
Brought to God their offering.
And His courts surrounding
Hear, in joy abounding,
   Happy throngs
   Singing songs,

With a mighty sounding.
(Repeat last 3 lines.)

Children of the Maccabees,
Whether free or fettered,
Wake the echoes of the songs,
Where you may be scattered.
Yours the message cheering
That the time is nearing
Which will see
All men free,
Tyrants disappearing.
(Repeat last 3 lines.)

ADAPTED FROM
GUSTAV GOTTHEIL AND M. JASTROW.